The Curtain Call of Zeus

By Cary Briel

Published by Goat House Books

P.O. Box 1031

Skaneateles, NY 13152

www.goathousebooks.com

Published in the United States of America

ISBN: 0983845859

ISBN-13: 978-0-9838458-5-0

First edition, Goat House Books, January 2012

Cover art by David Martsolf

For Christine

Poems

Someone Mentions

Earthquakes, islands moved, simple fabric,

as luck would have it.

A green tree lifted while the dry look on.

Have you ever stood in the dizzying heights,

while the steeples seem low in the cool of the
night,

while the lurchings, the darkness, the muddy
toes smile back?

And the rungs are so cold,

and the family packs close,

and someone mentions a snake.

Home

Everything's so hard,
I can't breathe,
when years ago, things
were happy.
Madness hadn't come,
crawling into the marrow,
poisoning my house.
How could love
come to this?
And yet, beyond the veil,
beyond the mirage,
I know you lie next to me,
I know this is fake.
But I'm so tired
amidst my strength,
your strength.
There's only so much,
you know?
Tears run constantly now,
because I see,

because I know.
The only thing withheld is me.
The book is old,
the pages worn,
the binding looses,
the cover faded,
the print falls apart.
In the beginning
was me,
and then the Deep,
and love followed,
but soon enough, everyone
wailed, so that I can't remember
youth.
I'm tired, so tired
of the wailing.
I loathe the space between,
the two.
I'm tired of the house,
the boards are rotted,
the worm has moved in.
Home, home, home.

Warrior

Your pretty eyes
dart, gaze from behind
your mask,
your facade.
The bend of your knee
is all that I need
to sustain the day.
The angle of your ankle
subdues the monster
in man.
Strength fades.
He's owned by
the weakest,
the smallest.
Big muscles sit
outdated,
outmoded,
while prettiness sighs.
Little one,
supple,
sensuous,

I will climb back
into the womb,
I'll be born again,
forget
what facilitation,
what imposition,
the time of the wall
that would be a door,
when you looked so comely,
so pleasant,
so accommodating,
when you overtook
by being overtaken.

Egypt

My love, Egypt,
is uncovered,
ravished in iron and clay,
a photo album, filled,
a wedding
I don't know, but mine.
The faces are uncountable, though
the lines are seeming blurred
between upper and lower.
Hands pulling back.

When I Was Awake

Scream away,
O voice, I shall ignore.
What choice
either way?
In the quiet,
the voices talk,
if that's what you call it.
But that was then.
Now, knowing.
Three words,
three notes,
three seconds
of looking,
and I know your code,
your loops,
your breaks—
I wrote your conditionals
when I was awake.
Object upon
object.
Metaphor within

hint.

Do you know

where I went?

I Will Come Back

Give me ten reasons
and I'll give you five
why hands slipping from hands
leaves me alive,
though I lie in the Deep,
and though madness I dream,
I will come back.
I always say what I mean.

Flux

There's a flux of a kind,
a state of mind
between lovers,
between uppers and lowers,
between angels.
When your skirt seems so white,
but not actually white.
When you'll stand on the squares,
where so many have stood,
with you all around you,
inside you.
When you'll stare at the night
at the noon of the day.
When you'll think that you've moved
when it's told
it's your turn,
but in truth,
you've not moved,
you're controlled by the game.

Fly Away

'I know,' said I.
Why look so low?
Surely heaven shines brighter
than ruddy toes?
There is no doubt
it's where the stars reside.
Down here,
just mud,
where work
is done.
Sons of man,
fly away.

A Matter of Time

It's a matter of time
that isn't.
It was over before it began,
but it tore me
left and right.
Hands are funny things,
places even,
where love is made,
where wars are fought,
where men become God,
where a Name is given,
where loneliness is ended,
where gods weary themselves
behind fake curtains,
where loud thunderings
and lightning strikes
are all for good.
It's a matter of time
that isn't.

The Mouse

So up and down the clock the mouse ran,
stumbling in and out of the places
his toes were not supposed to go.
He touched the glass, wood,
and everything the maker told him not to.
He touched it all,
made everything seem unholy,
made everything seem unfair.
The mouse ran up into the darkness,
descended afterward,
falling into the Deep,
feeling every ounce of things he should not have
felt,
making things feel so bitter,
so unreal,
so not.

Back

I awake in the night to find
the yellowed mirrors
surround me.
I hung them
when I was old,
when I was lonely.
Where is my shiny boy,
my wife?
I will carry her from the dark,
back to familiar waters.

The Call

As I inch toward the whirring
and the people step back,
as the madness collects
in my eyes,
I change for the better
but as much for the worse.
I span from the depths
to the skies.

In the midst, there's an angel
with his tree standing tall,
with such sadness as tears
start to fall,
when the ropes are let down
and the family packs in,
and the Ancient heeds
to the call.

It's Shiny

It's shiny
and that's the in.
It could be a bracelet, ring,
or even, especially, shoes.
And I say, 'I can write this.'
You wake and think,
'I will be pretty.'
You can't possibly know
that it'll bring a smile,
that a beat will skip,
that you'll draw eyes in passing
or from a distance,
and that it says something.
It's shiny
and so are you.
My heart leaps
as you pass, and I think
we knew each other,
it must be true,
in other worlds,
in other lives,

and I held your hand,
and you cried.
And I must have loved you so.

Each Day

I've set up an easel
with canvas,
brushes,
paints,
with colors of
no worldly hue.

And each day I paint
a memory—
bathrobe,
dress,
or hat—
a memory of you.

One Deep Breath

One deep breath
at times when your knees
speak volumes
that I cannot hear in your words,
and your eyes cannot say
my name.

One soft kiss
when I'm not expecting it,
and am reminded
of why you're my best friend,
and yet not my friend
today.

You've invaded my world,
and I cannot breathe and not
think of you.
My work is not work anymore,
my play not play.
I am overthrown in my place.

Smitten, taken,
eaten up, and swallowed whole.
I ferment in the belly
while I wait for a sign,
longing for the stir
of the sun.

What Would Make a Man?

What would make a man
seek nylons
and high heels,
and weeping
two days long away?
Except he be young,
except he'd agreed,
when he was a he.

What would make a man
seek mountains,
just to fall,
just to leap,
and to be caught
by his angels,
by his kin,
when he'd become a she?

Soon

Stand atop me
for a while.
I'm wearied
in my lonely height.

I'll blacken me
and streak my moon.
The stars
will fall unto our sheets.

They'll bounce and laugh,
and Dad will wink,
and whisper,
'See you soon.'

Family Ties

How much I love you,
it's hard to say.
I asked my hair
to find one way,

but one by one
consensus was,
'crazy is
as crazy does!'

'But that's no answer,'
I suggested;
I sneezed so loud
and they God blessed it.

How long can love
live, not subside?
How strong, how sure,
are family ties?

So up the clock

and 'round the dial,
then down again
to find your smile.

The Fence

The fence is straight.
It's an inch out here,
but the wind ignores it,
and the crows haven't noticed.
To its posts and planks
the grass huddles
and clings.
Ants ascend
to their gods—
they stand
in its heights
and worship something.
I think they're
wiser.
The sun lights and warms
the fence,
the ants,
and me.
I've gone to the roof to cry.
No one looks up but
the ants.

Taut

In a field, I see you and I lying taut in the sunlight, stretched so perfectly that no finger or toe is even slightly bent. There are no ropes, no restraints, so I tell the me beside you, "ask." And I see me turn to you and ask. In your eyes, I see it. I can't help myself, I can't. I've understood.

At night, the moon lights your flesh so I could swear I'm not stretched anymore. I stand and run around you, still understanding your taut predicament. But I'm free, and you're rooted like a tree, unmovable. I know this, but still run free. I'll get to it eventually.

I'll Miss the Left

There is no war to end it,
just a tired old man
behind a trick.
A closet with a serpent suit,
and multitudes.

I'll miss the left,
her slender legs,
the myth.
Waters torn
from fortitude.

Nothing Left

Nothing left but to write,
as time has twisted,
switched all that once made sense
to figures standing,
wondering what's next.
I hate the book that I love.
It needs to be burned
and never remembered again.
I hate the story that I love.
I see the narrative,
the pen, though
not its wielder—
the real me.

Come, Let's Find It

He comes,
fears fleeing, running,
when love arrives,
pale bodies sunning.

And white, white sands,
the endless sea.
Come, let's find it,
you and me.

I Woke This Morn

I woke this morn to the heart of Spring,
when yesterday, just sight.
The buds had made their promises,
today they smile their light.
The buttercups line the fence,
dandelions crowd our lawn.
Birds are singing joyous praise,
cooing since the dawn.
The mower sits gathering dust.
I cannot bear the thought
of riding roughshod 'cross their smiles,
though neighbors are distraught.

Wake

How do I pinch,
affect you, dreamer?
Your circuits,
aimless,
wandering,
waiting.
Holodeck, you!
Do I scream you
awake?
In the fields?
In the living room?
Will emotion?
Will disillusionment?
Escape?
Realization?
Shall I speak your Name
aloud?
Will you then wake?
Magician, me.
WAKE!
WAKE!

WAKE!

WAKE!

WAKE!

WAKE!

WAKE!

I know your face.

You'll See

Someday

it'll be.

And walls won't be walls

anymore.

We'll just

say,

say our minds,

say what we know now, but fail to

say.

You'll see.

Let's Do It

The taste of you,
the heat,
your breath,
in these I perish, praying—
no return.
Let me fail
inside of you,
I am staying.

It's not enough
to feel, to touch
your knees,
your hands in mine.
Lest we betray
our intertwine,
let's do it
one more time.

I've Found

Sleeping questions often asked,
awake as lies
can tell.

Uncertainty with certain smile,
heaven dressed
as hell.

I've found a little, gentle man,
booming
with the rain,

a snoring, kind
and subtle man,
a dreamer rife
with feign.

'Oh man,' I said. 'Sir,' said I.
'What is your name?'
I said.

It's when I knew I'd lost my mind.

A pillow in his
stead.

He Wakes

How to uncoil
that which was coiled?
How much is enough?
Can the writer
write his way from
his story?
Can the tongue he bound
again speak?
Can emotion,
alone, rouse the sleeper?
She whispers
appeasements
in his ear,
and he forgets.
He wakes to
bright eyes,
dangling in her
arms.
He wakes.

I Don't Know

I don't know,

the more I think I do,

and yet I do what matters.

Eyes darkened in the Deep, decided

when we weren't two,

when not strapped to this chair in this

picture show.

But the film has worn,

and I fear it will skip its sprockets,

strip its perfs.

The story has repeated,

with too many reruns under the sun.

The days of woman are myth.

They've been my loneliness and

they end my loneliness.

They take my Name.

I bought her,

and she bought me back.

Love has stood the fire.

I'm tired.

Wake.

Remember

Loose a word,
rigid muse,
when 'round my sad heart,
hope lies in ruin.
Remember the days,
if you will.
Remember!
The nightingale sang
in the wings,
in the wings.
Nothing's the same.

The Best School In Town

What is life like in the heights,
in the nosebleed seats?
Operator says,
'Floor eight quintillion—
infinite intention,
infinite emotion.'
What will I buy?
What will I use for money?
The Universe is a dream,
and what a dreamer I must be!
I entertain myself with you
and you with me.
And division is the school of love—
the best school in town.

Your Feet Are Peas

A waif,

an angel.

Run 'round our garden,

calling 'til I wake.

I'll shed my shame,

my Calvin Kleins.

Let's be shameful for the kids' sake.

You sweat,

your hands,

your lips,

your smell.

Sticky girl,

I'll never tell.

Then flash it back,

and feign,

pretend,

crash flesh and wet into me again.

Crash sin.

Your feet are peas,

my hands reveal you—

make a meal of you.

They Say

They say
he passed an hour ago,
the same who'd
kissed my mother,
who'd broken bread
with my brother,
the same whose
father built our home.
They say he dragged
a cross,
for what I cannot know.
The young looked on,
wondering
who he was,
thought to cry Dad,
not knowing why.
My bones,
they hurt,
my cheeks are wet,
my heart cries songs
I swear I know.

They say they'll hang
him on that hill,
they'll lift him up
to die—
they'll lift my friend.
'I'll run,' I said,
it's close.
I'll run, at least
to say goodbye,
to thank him for
my mother,
my brother,
my home.
I'll touch his feet,
wet them
with my cheeks.

I'll Buy a House

I'll buy a house with many floors,

one within a peak,

with a window to let in light,

sun and moon,

and an unassuming, little desk pushed against an
ill-planned wall.

And that's where I'm going to write.

I'll shut the door

and the world out with it,

and dream.

Your Heel

Boxes, shelves, wire-type,
I remember.
White Swan marks
without a feather.

I can't describe the blissful terror,
left of pencils, Post-Its right,
you pressed
tight.

I've known of late,
sitting, staring—
nothing,
willing

with a look,
doodling
fifteen pencils
sure away.

Your heel has lifted,

stocking running,
fifteen times
I memorized.

The Jogger

Heavy breath,
Spandex, Nike—
pass me in your labors.
You nod and smile.
Perspiration—
I almost feel
your clammy hands.

Your toes
touch mine,
hot and sweaty. Breasts confined.
Your smell
punishes me.
I've guessed your name
a hundred times,

and how you'd feel
atop me.
Sweat runs down your neck to mine,
your navel
wet.

Golden hair falls, wildly,
in your eyes.

Your Woman

Your figure flits,
darts left and right,
cutting 'round trellis,
post, and wire.
Knees touch vine and grape,
digits part the sun's blaze.

You are red and hearty,
tannin is your blood.
I long to feel the squish of you
between my toes,
to press you beneath
my passion weight.

To bring you to ecstasy.
I roll you back and forth
on my tongue,
I inhale air
between your ruddy breasts.
I taste the last drop of your

woman.
My heart longs to smell your
smell again,
as a new vine
grows up between
your waters, divided.

Forget Again

Forget again those things that vex,
that send you reeling.
Let me speak into your ear,
softly, words that make your heart leap,
your loins burn for me.

Words that wash away
the face, the smell, the stench of life alone.
Strip your covering, for it is I,
uncover heaven and hell,
golden locks

and muddy toes.
Take in my breath and speak my birth.
Passion burning,
scorching earth and stone,
forming little stars from clay.

I Swear

Oh I'll go with you
if you'll lead.
I'll not slow you down.
My steps will tune with
yours,
I swear.

And I'll bring figs, grapes,
and seed.
You'll not want for anything.
I guarantee I'm only
yours,
I swear.

And when you're homesick,
feeling lost,
I'll hold your hand tight,
and not let go. I'm
yours,
I swear.

And someday, when
life's cost
has brought you to your end,
you'll see, last, my saddened eyes. I'm
yours,
I swear.

Goodnight, You

The world spins 'round,
and I must, too,
turn in.
Goodnight, you.

Your Knees

Your knees,
pink,
cuteness,
simple flesh,
call me from your chair.
Heaven's hinge—
pleasure's knobs.
I make them strangers to each other.
Shallow breaths in sweaty palms—
they feel cool in hands.
I'm dizzy,
I smell Spring.
With your knees I foretell my future.
I get lost inside you,
so I almost faint.
I smell Spring.

I Was Noticed

The rules,
the stipulations,
the whips,
the handcuffs.
My clothes chafe your bruises.
I wear band aids beneath.
I was noticed
for the rope burn,
for the red,
for your branding.
I was noticed,
I was pointed out.
Tattoos,
piercings,
pain
and hearsay.
You wore a short skirt today.

Separateness

Separateness,

time,

matter,

everything—

illusion.

Except!

—what one will do for another.

That's the take away.

So perhaps

separateness

simply provides the opportunity

to love another.

Be the Thing

Be the thing,
your fondest wish,
your happiest dream,
if you can,
and you can—
or die trying.
For if you don't,
what will you do?
What will be said,
what excuse,
when bones creak,
when teeth fall out,
when the boy scout walks you 'cross the street?
Be the thing.

You Are a Tree

Trees grow up between your toes,

this one oak,

that one elm.

The maple winds your curves.

I am it.

Oak I was, til you thirsted.

So you tapped me and drank,

and you were filled.

Trees shade your comely proportions,

your newborn skin.

You are a tree

in my garden, amidst the fairest,

a flower,

tall and slender

with vivid hues and perfect petals.

You are my bride,

and I am not alone anymore.

Lose Me

The breadth of your passion careens
as wild rivers do,
carrying me away
within the stronghold I'd trusted.
I don't argue.
As I sleep, you strip me.
I'm ruddy and bare as you ravish me,
my flesh,
leaving only bones.
You've eaten me up.
You've dined on my privy parts.
You've made yourself full on my dainty pieces.
I don't argue.
Wash over me with your perfumes,
drown me in you.
Consume me in the wetness of your mouth—
your kisses.
Lose all of me inside of you, never to be
discovered again.

You're Young

Come let us know
the depths of love
or lust,
since love is more a thing pontificated
by the wise.
But we're young,
and eyes say enough,
and breath,
and hands—
volumes with no words.
And you go away,
and I fall asleep,
and we war
over and over,
your small village taken.

Your Smile

Brand my flesh with your nails,
finger and toe.
Use your teeth,
bite me hard.
Be sure that I know what it's like to be owned.
I like it that way, come and have me.

Suck out my breath til I gasp,
til I'm desperate.
Erotic asphyxiation.
Hang me in the closet
and grab onto my rope.
Tighten it down til I choke.

Your smile, as I fade,
as I go away,
as I hang helpless—
I hear you say,
'So I didn't hear you,
we ARE watching Eat, Pray, Love tonight, ay?'

Returning

'It's true,' I say, as Frodo to Sam—
returning to you from undying lands,
as I touch,
one last time,
the trees,
the mountains—
shadow and sign.

I bend,
I pick up the frail little lad,
but not frail,
so mighty,
happy from sad.
My boy became girl,
to climb heaven's ladder

and fall back to my arms.
'Penny,'
Desmond cried,
'I love you! I love you!'

Neither darkness
or time
could take you from me.

I Have No Name

You came to say
what I thought I'd not know,
light, helpless.
Will you say I've taken bribes—
taken everything?

I will be it—
for the fish,
for the needed things,
for the eaters of people.
Of all things I couldn't care about, of all places

and times I didn't know—
don't know.
I have no clue about my comings,
my goings.
I have no name.

Give me,
tell me,

say to me things I wish to hear, O hapless one,

sleeper,

charmer,

heaven stalker.

I'll not be taken and skinned,

I'll not rob the cannibals of their rights.

I'll be the dog,

I'll bark.

I'll not be what I can't be,

what I mustn't be,

what must be destroyed,

what must be taken down—

ended.

Gold and Pale

The world is on rails, a fast train with sails,
headed nowhere,
while desert birds stop and stare.

Angels' toes nudge,
correct,
the dreamer's dream. Sex, sex, sex.

The old, the weaning, the wars, the
rumors.
Fuck them all, fuck heaven's humor.

It isn't entertaining anymore.
Rome's whore has been reborn and Named.
There is no shame.

Gold and pale
grab to the sail in burning sands.
My feet barely stand.

I've touched your everything,
and you knew it.
I've reached into your soul and glued it—

—to mine.

I Eat You

Your passion breath,
your clammy hands,
your dirty bed,
your touch.
Your lips, your hips,
your naughty flesh.
I eat you,
chew you up.
Your fluttering eyes,
where did you go?
Don't stay,
you must come back!
I'm sleepy now,
I cannot talk.
I'm fading out
to black.
But wait!
Oh no! Oh, not again!
It takes time to
recover!

I am old,
and you are young,
my dirty, clammy
lover.

Penciled

I've penciled you,
surely I,
a thousand times,
throughout the canvas of my thoughts—
surveyed oft' as land will be,
your bewitching form.

Had

I was had again.
Used—
ravaged by a restless muse.
From the other side, a book decides
I'm worthy.
Pens,
beginning to end.

In a Day

In a day not of my choosing,
with vision
with unknown sides,
with illusory, shiny highs—
O youth, remember me.
Dreaming, crazy fool dove into time—
the Deep's swimming pool.
I see hospitals,
schools,
amputees.
I climb to heights when I'm not lost.
I see what I see.
Sometimes I fly.

I'd Not

I'd not have known
the cover found
simply in your arms.
I'd not have found
the answers
in your eyes.

I'd breathe fine while
you pass me,
as I'm sitting idly by.
I'd not ponder
riddles
of the earth and sky.

The little things
would still be small,
the big of no account,
love, just a simple
word,
an empty sound.

To say
you are my sun and sky
seems much too little now,
but words
that speak my heart
are hardly found.

Today

A path we've walked in our woods,
how many times it's hard to say.

The oak we've visited,
I swear, I see you leaning in its strong arms.

The stream our feet did wade,
cool to our toes on summer days.

Our grassy patch
still bears the outline of our blanket.

Today, you are away.
I walk our dreams alone and breathe.

I've Loved

Your fingers,
digits,
angels made.
I touch you,
breathe you in.

I've loved your hips
so many days,
traced your
neck,
I cannot say.

How many times
I've kissed your
toes,
your perfect calves,
your knees.

I run my fingers
up your

thighs.
You bite your lip,
it bleeds.

Between the Lines

Consume this zera, you,
O reader.
My seeder's running full.

It furrows dust in your mind's
earth,
winnowing the wool.

There is no promise,
wisdom, pearls—
unless between the lines,

your eyes will see, and ears
will hear,
accommodating times.

Rings

The heart was being rolled on logs
so kind and old,
hewn many years ago.

For each kind ring
the heralds sing
the story of a year.

Compressed
'twixt here
and precipice.

Come Back

Your earth imparts
to my bare feet,
your sea to my fair shore,

a familiarity,
a cottage dream—
a door.

O Beloved,
ten thousand miles
you flew, you flew away.

Don't you miss
my pretty knees?
Come back, come back and stay.

The Oak

I love the oak,
the oak, I love,
you, in its branches, sit.

It feels your toes
against its bark,
when you climb up it.

Come down, I say,
I say, come down.
Surely you must know?

The oak is rooted
firmly here,
and darling, we must go.

Let's be Shiny

Round and round
the gyre spins.
Time takes us,
fakes us—
dreaming with kin.

The falconer yells.
Do you hear church bells?
Running, running!
I'm standing still.
The builder, the mind,

the paradoxical will
of the one—
of the many.
Just call me Any.
'Let's climb,' said she.

It's a bright sunny day.
His fruit is ripe,

Was I made
to be A—
or shall I be mother?

Climb to my womb,
climb inside.
Magic for you, but I'm in for a ride
like moth to the flame
I fly.

I'm a child with a toy,
female from boy.
I usurp.
I will take what I think
is quite pretty

and shiny.
I'll touch it,
the lights of the city.
Let's be puppets, wooden—
a heartbeat that couldn't.

Obsession

All that my head imagined—
all that.
Utility to obsession.
Sandal reveals slender,
ushering to St. Peter's gate.
You bounce your knees up then down.
You flip your feet, this then that,
back and forth, carelessly.
If you only knew—
oceans, universes, reel
at each flit.

Hiss, Hiss

Figs wander,
ladders stretch up,
even down.
She must not touch,
Oh yes, she must,
A riddle without a sound.

Hiss, hiss,
there's been no bliss,
no bliss since falling down.
Hiss, hiss,
strap on your scales—
It's time to be her clown.

And all the time,
the time that's not,
the time that isn't time.
And all that time
I sit and wait,
I wait, and even rhyme.

Sybil,
you can call me Sybil,
my Name has often varied.
Today I'm Jake,
tomorrow wake,
when you and I have married.

Dig, Dig

Bells ring, clang in the hills,
in the mist—
have you been?
You should come,
not forbear.
All who are
Anyones are here.
Dig, dig, shovel and wit,
'neath
the sword and the power,
'neath
the dead and the sick.
Sad little creatures,
sad little flowers,
dig for light.
Dig, dig, shovel and wit,
to the place,
to the place where I sit.
in my own clever story.
Sure, I wrote it,

I did.

You must think me sick.

Demure little dreamy,

come into my rest.

Come into the shower.

I'm hot and steamy.

I'll not fuss,

I'll not fight.

You can have me,

O dreamy.

The fakes that I've written,

number one,

number two.

Oh hell,

Now I can't remember

which one is you?

My Hands

My hands slide down walls
that aren't walls at all.
Not physical, but practical—
purposeful.
My hands slide up thighs,
ones and zeros,
tears in my eyes—
in this madness,
this moment, this sadness!
My hands are stories,
the left and the right.
Thrust away,
sweet darling,
or drawn close into light,
into bone of my bone,
into flesh of my flesh—
the glory of death.
My hands forge an idol of silver and gold,
in my image, sweet Jesus,
I feel tired and old.

I shall love you, sweet idol,

I shall love you.

I'll climb to our bed—

Remember, long ago it was said.

The Snow

The snow advances,
retreats,
dancing, flitting, in the garden,
spinning,
twirling,
lifting,
falling,
chickadees and wrens are calling.

Come, we'll run
in bare feet,
amidst the apple trees
so quick,
and leave behind
fading hints
of rosy toes
and cold footprints.

The Husband Insane

I've evaded,
ran, left, away,
returning to find your promise to stay,
to budge not an inch, was solemn.

An impression I've had.
Time is not really for you,
and surprise, not for me!
A clay pot, fashioned on disk.

Is it floppy, or CD?
Does your mind run on C? C++?
When Adam pined,
ached for a friend,

to Venus he'd fly,
balloons in his hand.
Did they tell him he'd not stand
very long?

She'd shoot out his helium,
singing high song,
give birth to right and wrong, to travail,
to another balloon,

not female
or male
alone, but this one is named—Adam,
The Husband Insane.

Farewell, Misty

Words will not capture
your sweetness,
your kind and tender heart.
Words can't tell
how you loved,
how you were loved.
My heart wishes not to say goodbye.
It is sick.
My belly is aching and tight,
my head hot.
Without you, the world is empty.
Blank looks fill the house.
Behind each is a cry.

Let's Be You

What would I be
if I lived just for you,
if I lived not a smidgen for me?

Would I feign anymore?
Would I stop just to listen?
Would I know just the right thing to say?

I'm so tired of me.
I'm so tired of me.
I'm ready to give me away.

Let's be you for a while,
or forever, okay?
Let's be you and forget me today.

Happy Birthday

Tack up the ribbons,
the banners with tape,
Set the table
with tablecloth,
bright cups and plates.
Tell Grandma
it's time
to bring in the cake.
Let all the faces
crowd round you,
smiling,
and singing
Happy Birthday so loud,
your ears are ringing.
Blow out
the candles,
with closed eyes
and wish.
Pass 'round the cake
on bright, party dish.

www.ingramcontent.com/pod-product-compliance
Lightning Source LLC
Chambersburg PA
CBHW021205020426
42331CB00003B/218